ANDREW McCUTCHEN

NATIONAL LEAGUE
MVP

BY BRENDAN FLYNN

Published by The Child's World®
1980 Lookout Drive • Mankato, MN 56003-1705
800-599-READ • www.childsworld.com

ACKNOWLEDGMENTS
The Child's World®: Mary Berendes, Publishing Director
Red Line Editorial: Editorial direction
The Design Lab: Design
Amnet: Production
Design elements: Open Clip Art Library, 1, 3, 22
Photographs ©: Tony Gutierrez/AP Images, cover, 9, 17;
Bennett Cohen/Icon SMI, 5; Frank Franklin II/AP Images, 7;
Four Seam Images/AP Images, 11; John Heller/AP Images, 13;
Rich Graessle/Icon SMI, 15; Gene J. Puskar/AP Images, 19;
Helga Esteb/Shutterstock Images, 21

ISBN 9781631437342
LCCN 2014945304

Printed in the United States of America
Mankato, MN
November, 2014
PA02239

ABOUT THE AUTHOR
Brendan Flynn is a San Francisco resident and author of numerous children's books. Flynn also enjoys competing in triathlons, Scrabble tournaments, and chili cook-offs.

TABLE OF CONTENTS

CHAPTER 1

DEFENSIVE DYNAMO

The ball is hit. It sails toward a gap in right-center field. The runners hurry around the bases. Then a blur in a black uniform appears. Andrew McCutchen, center fielder for the Pittsburgh Pirates, is on the scene. McCutchen dives for the ball. He slides on his belly. The ball drops into his glove for an out. McCutchen and his teammates run off the field. The Pirates are on their way to another win.

McCutchen is one of the best players in Major League Baseball (MLB). He is strong and fast. And in 2013, he had the best season of any player in the National League (NL).

Baseball players are judged on five important skills, or "tools." Hitting for average. Hitting for power. Running. Throwing. Playing defense. McCutchen is excellent at all of them.

McCutchen dives for a catch against the New York Mets on May 27, 2014.

CHAPTER 2

EARLY YEARS

On October 10, 1986, Andrew Stefan McCutchen was born in Fort Meade, Florida. Both of Andrew's parents were great athletes. Andrew was very athletic, too.

But Andrew's parents didn't want him to focus on sports alone. They sent him to a private school called Union Academy. He developed interests in drawing and poetry. But Union didn't have a baseball team. So Andrew returned to Fort Meade public school for eighth grade.

Andrew's father, Lorenzo, attended Carson-Newman College on a football scholarship. His mother, Petrina, was an excellent volleyball player in high school.

McCutchen hits a single against the New York Mets on May 28, 2014.

CHAPTER 3

MULTISPORT STAR

Andrew made the Fort Meade High School varsity baseball team in eighth grade. He was the team's starting shortstop. He had a .591 **batting average** that season. That was better than any player in the county. Andrew moved to the outfield the next year. That position took advantage of his amazing speed. He went on to hit .474 over his high school career. As a senior, he hit over .700 and stole 45 bases.

Andrew once scored five touchdowns in a high school football game. He played wide receiver.

Andrew also ran track. He was part of a state championship 4x100-meter relay team. His football skills drew attention, too. Many colleges offered Andrew baseball and football scholarships. He decided he wanted to play baseball at the University of Florida.

Running track in high school gave McCutchen speed that came in handy running bases in the major leagues.

CHAPTER 4

CLIMBING THE LADDER

I n June 2005, McCutchen got a call from the Pittsburgh Pirates. They had selected him in the MLB **Draft**. He was the 11th player taken. McCutchen had an important decision to make. He had not yet enrolled at the University of Florida. But now he had an opportunity to start a professional baseball career. McCutchen decided to go pro. But he couldn't play for the Pirates just yet. McCutchen had to work his way up in the **minor leagues**.

McCutchen was rated the 14th-best **prospect** in the minor leagues by *Baseball America* magazine before the 2008 season.

McCutchen was an **All-Star** in the South Atlantic League in his first full season. The Pirates named him their Minor League Player of the Year. It was clear that McCutchen had a bright future with the Pirates.

McCutchen played outfield for the Hickory Crawdads in the minor leagues.

CHAPTER 5

BREAKING THROUGH

McCutchen rose through the minor leagues quickly. On June 3, 2009, the Pirates traded their center fielder. That opened a spot for McCutchen. The next day, he made his major league debut. McCutchen had an amazing first game. He got two hits, scored three runs, drove in a run, and stole a base. He showed everybody that he was ready to play in the big leagues.

Baseball America named McCutchen MLB Rookie of the Year after the 2009 season. He was named to the NL All-Star team in 2011 and 2012. But McCutchen yearned for team success. He had not yet helped the Pirates reach the playoffs.

> McCutchen led all of MLB with 194 hits in 2012. He finished third in the voting for the NL Most Valuable Player (MVP) Award that season.

McCutchen (left) celebrates with teammate Nyjer Morgan (right) after scoring against the New York Mets during McCutchen's first game on June 4, 2009.

CHAPTER 6

CHANGING FORTUNES

The Pirates were not a very good team when McCutchen joined them. They hadn't been to the playoffs since 1992. In 2010, they were the worst team in baseball. Then they started to improve. In 2012, they won almost as many games as they lost. But they would have to do better to reach the playoffs.

The Pirates started out strong in 2013. In late June they took over first place in their division. McCutchen was named to the NL All-Star team again. Fans loved watching him hit the ball hard and run the bases. They also loved watching him chase after fly balls. He was one of the most popular players in all of baseball.

McCutchen won a contest to be on the cover of the popular video game *MLB 13: The Show*. More than 100,000 fans voted for him.

McCutchen (right) slides safely into second base for the National League during the 2013 MLB All-Star Game.

CHAPTER 7

WINNING THE WILD CARD

The Pirates finished the 2013 season strong. They led their division for most of August. In late September they were tied for first place with the St. Louis Cardinals. But the Cardinals pulled ahead and won the division.

The Pirates were not done. They could still make the playoffs as a **wild card** team. And that is just what they did. The Pirates won six of their last eight games to clinch a spot in the playoffs. McCutchen finished the year with 21 home runs and 27 stolen bases. He had a .317 batting average.

McCutchen was six years old in 1992, the last time the Pirates had made the playoffs.

The Pittsburgh Pirates trade high fives following a 5-4 win over the Texas Rangers on September 10, 2013.

CHAPTER 8

PLAYOFF EXCITEMENT

Pittsburgh hosted the NL wild card game against the Cincinnati Reds. The loser would be done for the year. The Pirates won 6-2. McCutchen had two hits and scored a run. It was Pittsburgh's first playoff win in 21 years.

The Pirates now had to face the Cardinals. It was a five-game series. Pittsburgh won two of the first three games. But the Cardinals pulled out an exciting 2-1 win in Game 4. Then they won the last game 6-1. The Pirates' season was over. But what a season it had been!

The Cardinals lost the 2013 World Series to the Boston Red Sox.

McCutchen takes off after a hit against the Cincinnati Reds in the wild card game on October 1, 2013.

CHAPTER 9

A TROPHY AND A RING

McCutchen was named the NL MVP. He received 28 of the 30 first-place votes. He was the first Pirate to win the award since Barry Bonds in 1992. He also won his second straight Silver Slugger award. That goes to the best hitter at each position on the field in each league.

But the awards were just one part of McCutchen's big off-season. In December, he proposed to his longtime girlfriend, Maria Hanslovan. He was a guest on *Ellen* that day. Host Ellen DeGeneres called Hanslovan up on stage. McCutchen gave Hanslovan a diamond ring. She said yes.

McCutchen keeps busy during the winter. He does lots of work for his favorite charities around Pittsburgh. And he

> McCutchen gives much of his free time to charity. He is involved with Habitat for Humanity and the Children's Hospital of Pittsburgh.

prepares hard for the next season. McCutchen has already helped end the Pirates' long playoff drought. Now he hopes to lead the Pirates to their first World Series since 1979.

McCutchen with fiancé Maria Hanslovan at the American Music Awards on November 24, 2013

FUN FACTS

ANDREW MCCUTCHEN

BORN: October 10, 1986

HOMETOWN: Fort Meade, Florida

TEAMS: Pittsburgh Pirates (2009–)

POSITION: Center fielder

HEIGHT: 5'11"

WEIGHT: 190 pounds

MAJOR LEAGUE DEBUT: June 4, 2009

PLAYOFF APPEARANCES: 2013

ALL-STAR APPEARANCES: 2011, 2012, 2013, 2014

AWARDS

  NL MVP: 2013

  SILVER SLUGGER: 2012, 2013

GLOSSARY

All-Star (AWL stahr) A player who is named one of the best in his league is an All-Star. McCutchen was named an All-Star for the first time in 2011.

batting average (BAT-ing AV-ur-ij) Batting average is a statistic that measures how often a player gets a base hit. McCutchen had a .327 batting average in the 2012 season.

draft (draft) Professional teams scout and select new players to join their rosters in the draft. The Pirates selected McCutchen 11th overall in the 2005 MLB Draft.

minor leagues (MYE-nur leegz) The minor leagues are a lower level of baseball where players work on improving their skills before they reach the major leagues. McCutchen was a star in the minor leagues.

prospect (PRAHS-pekt) A prospect is a young player who has a good chance of becoming a superstar. McCutchen was a top prospect in the minor leagues.

wild card (wilde kahrd) A wild card team is a team that did not win its division but still had a good enough record to qualify for the playoffs. The Pirates made the playoffs as a wild card team in 2013.

TO LEARN MORE

BOOKS

LeBoutillier, Nate. *The Story of the Pittsburgh Pirates (Baseball: The Great American Game)*. Mankato, MN: Creative Paperbacks, 2012.

Pittsburgh Post-Gazette. *Revival by the River: The Resurgence of the Pittsburgh Pirates*. Chicago, IL: Triumph Books, 2013.

WEB SITES

Visit our Web site for links about Andrew McCutchen:
childsworld.com/links

Note to Parents, Teachers, and Librarians: We routinely verify our Web links to make sure they are safe and active sites. So encourage your readers to check them out!

INDEX